Dominating the skyline at this Banbury Fair is the Big Wheel. With the coming of the traction engine, electricity became available to the showman to light up his ride. Owners of Big Wheels took advantage of this to plaster lights all over them. Big Wheels then became a blaze of light in the sky and were usually placed near the edge of a fair to act as a beacon to attract the crowds. This photograph, taken at the turn of the century, shows a Wheel before it was covered in electric light bulbs. One of the snags of a Wheel is that each of the suspended chairs has to be loaded and unloaded singly. This takes time, with the result that the Big Wheels are unlikely to take as much money per hour as say, a set of Gallopers or Dodgems. The lady in the bottom left-hand corner is dressed in the typical costume of an Oxfordshire traveller.

HISTORIC FAIRGROUND SCENES

Michael E. Ware FRPS

MOORLAND PUBLISHING COMPANY

COPYRIGHT NOTICE

Printed in Great Britain by
Wood Mitchell & Co Ltd, Stoke-on-Trent

For the Publishers
Moorland Publishing Company
The Market Place, Hartington,
Buxton, Derbys, SK17 0AL

Contents

Acknowledgements

There is a wealth of photographs of fairground subjects in private and public collections throughout the country. For some strange reason the quality of these photographs is usually very poor indeed, and many excellent subjects have had to be rejected due to the fact that they will just not reproduce in a book such as this. I must have considered over 10,000 photographs in order to select the hundred and twenty or so which appear in these pages, and to those many people who have let me browse for hours through their collections, only to find I have used only one or two, I would like to say a special thank you. I have consulted many Public Libraries and Museums, finding the staff very helpful indeed. I would like to single out the great help given to me by Jack Wilkinson, known to many as the 'Cyclist' in *World's Fair*. Jack spent many hours reading my captions and then adding his own comments. In some cases these were so detailed that it was quite impossible to incorporate all the information given.

To my friend and near neighbour Arthur Hosey who spent most of his life with Arnold Brothers' fair must go a sincere vote of thanks for allowing me the full use of his collection of photographs and for providing me with so much background information. He too added a great number of facts to my researched material. I am pleased to say that Arthur is still closely connected with preservation, and attends many traction engine rallies each year with his caravan displaying several hundred of his fairground photographs. Much information has been gleaned from the large library of books on both the circus and the fair owned by John Pocock of Berwick St John, who kindly lent me all these for well over a year. Lesley Harnett typed dozens of letters and the manuscript while Michael Sedgwick read the manuscript and proofs and gave much advice.

The author and publisher are grateful to the following for the use of illustrations:
Banbury Library: *frontis*; Author's Collection: 1, 10, 98, 101, 102; South Tyneside Public Library: 2, 36; Benjamin Stone Collection, Birmingham City Library: 3, 12, 49, 50; Radio Times Hulton Picture Library: 4, 5, 7, 11, 13, 23, 37, 51, 52, 62, 64, 67, 74, 76, 78, 79, 80, 99, 112, 116, 117, 119, 120; Oxford City Library: 6, 24, 31, 47, 55, 69, 83; Hertfordshire County Records Office: 8; A. Hosey: 9, 17, 19, 20, 25, 26, 29, 30, 32, 35, 42, 43, 44, 45, 46, 66, 73, 84, 85, 87, 89, 90, 91, 92, 93, 100, 103, 105, 106, 114; Laing Art Gallery & Museum, Newcastle-upon-Tyne: 14, 21, 38, 40, 53, 56, 57, 58, 81, 82, 107, 108, 109, 111, 113; Nottingham Historical Film Unit: 15, 16, 28, 41, 54, 70, 95, 96; Mansell Collection: 18, 59, 60, 72, 94, 118; National Motor Museum: 22, 88; Jack Wilkinson: 27, 34, 75, 86, 97; *Old Motor*: 33, 104; Greater London Council: 39; Devon Library Service (Torquay): 48; Liverpool Public Library: 61, 121; Kodak Museum: 63; Central Library Norwich: 65; John Carter: 68, 77, 115; Victoria & Albert Museum: 71; Birmingham CIty Library Collection: 110.

Introduction

The fair is not a recent phenomenon. Its origins can be traced back to Roman times, the word fair deriving from the Latin for holiday — *feria*. The earliest fairs were for trade — an extension of the market place. Some specialised in the sale of animals; we have horse fairs, sheep fairs, pony fairs and goose fairs, and there was even one at Yarmouth for the herring. Whenever one found a group of people gathered for this type of trade or barter, inevitably there were itinerant traders and with them travelling entertainers such as acrobats, jugglers and fortune tellers.

As fairs became more popular some were legalised and given a charter; records exist of chartered fairs in Norman times. One of the most interesting types of fair is the hiring fair, always held in the autumn. These were large outdoor labour exchanges to which labourers and craftsmen came in search of employment. They paraded through the fair wearing in their lapels or on their caps tokens of their jobs; carters displayed pieces of whip-cord, maids carried mops and these soon became known as mop fairs. A few weeks later another similar fair was often held called the runaway mop, this latter giving those still unemployed a second chance to fix themselves up before the winter. It also gave employers the chance to change any staff that had already proved unsatisfactory.

The travelling fair as we know it today could not come into existence until there were roads good enough to cope with heavy loads. Before the Turnpike Road Acts of 1730 and 1780, the roads of Great Britain were in an appalling condition. For example, it took six horses to draw a small stage coach, and in winter many roads were impassable due to mud. Thomas Telford and John Macadam were the prime movers in road building and surfacing in the 1820s. Until these better roads were made, those travelling from fair to fair usually went on foot or horseback, though wealthier ones might own enough horses to pull a cart. They slept in roadside inns or tents, or slept rough; the caravan did not become popular until roads were improved. With the better highways came greater loads, and the travelling showman with his large sideshows, menageries and elaborate rides was born.

Throughout the nineteenth century the travelling fair developed. First sideshows got bigger, and then came the rides. At first these were hand-driven, but in the latter part of the century steam revolutionised the traditional fairground, being used to power roundabouts and other rides. It was also applied as a prime mover on the road. Electricity then brightened the scene.

In 1874 Thomas Frost wrote this of the travelling fairs: '. . . the railways connect the smaller towns, and most of the villages, with the larger ones in which amusements may be found superior to any ever presented by the old showman. What need then of fairs and shows? The nation has outgrown them, and the last showman will soon be as great a curiosity as the dodo.' Frost had got it wrong, for transport was not as yet readily available — to the working classes at any rate. Tradition dies hard; most of the established town fairs kept going, while the country fair had a place all to itself in the lives of the younger people of the villages. The author can still remember the annual fair and the carnival as being two of the highspots in the life of his native village.

The showmen adapted to the changing ways, presenting only those rides and shows not found in the local town amusement park. As the zoo and the circus became more popular, the travelling menagerie died out. The theatre became established in permanent buildings, so killing off the travelling theatre. Picture palaces became common, so the Bioscope show was relegated to the past. In more recent years the traditional Roundabout lost favour, youngsters preferring the thrills of the Ark or Waltzer or the more modern Jets, Looper or Paratrooper. The Dodgems introduced in the 1920s are still popular, but the cars themselves have to be continually updated to keep in fashion.

Yesterday's rides have not entirely disappeared; there are still a few sets of Galloping Horses (some steam-driven) and Cakewalks. There is even a set of Steam Yachts, too. Although these rides attend a few of the major fairs, most of their time is spent at traction engine rallies and other similar events for 'preserved' transport. Many attempts have been made to re-create the atmosphere of the old-time fair as shown in this book following the highly successful event staged at Shottesbrooke Park, White Waltham, in August 1964, but at the time of writing that pioneer classic has never been surpassed.

This book attempts to depict the fairground from the mid 1860s, a time when a few enterprising photographers turned their cameras onto the social scene, up to the outbreak of World War II. During this period we saw the heyday of the fairground; steam came in to transform the rides, but then declined with the rise of the diesel lorry and generator: inevitably, some of the glamour was lost.

1 One of the origins of the fair as we know it today was the traditional horse fair. A few years ago it looked as if they were likely to disappear but quite a number of these events have survived up and down the country and are enjoying a new lease of life. Perhaps the largest of all the horse fairs is the one staged on the outskirts of Appleby, Cumbria, during June. This is attended by dealers from a very wide area. Another important one is Lee Gap Fair at West Ardsley, outside Wakefield. This is held on St Bartholomew's Day (24 August) and is followed three weeks and three days later by a similar one-day horse fair. At one time Lee Gap Fair lasted for the whole period, but now only the first and last days are observed, so the fairs are known as 'First Lee' and 'Latter Lee'. The fair shown in this photograph was being held at Alfreton around the turn of the century.

SOUTH SHIELDS MARKET PLACE. 302.

2 The earliest fairs were in the market place, and many have traditionally retained the same sites. Sites such as this present problems to showmen, as on many occasions they cannot take up their positions until after the market has closed and the stalls have been cleared away, at say six o'clock in the evening. The fair has then to be assembled rapidly in order to open the following day. However, at South Shields in 1899 the fair has come to the market place, leaving the market traders to carry on their regular business around the fringes.

3 Sir Benjamin Stone photographed these three labourers at Stratford-upon-Avon Mop Fair in 1899. All are wearing tokens of their trade indicating that they are looking for employment.

4 and 5 Two photographs of labourers seeking employment, taken as late as autumn 1912 at the hiring fair at High Wycombe.

4

5

The Tober

6

6 The appearance of the tober or fairground has changed a great deal over the years. This is St Giles Fair, Oxford, in 1868. The showmens' living wagons line St Giles on the left with the stalls facing the pavement, while on the right of the street are the shows and the menageries. St Giles Fair has no charter; it grew out of a much smaller event, the annual Wake of Walton Parish. It is still held every year, on the same site and in nearby Magdalen Street, on the Monday and Tuesday following the first Sunday in September. Until a few years ago the showmen were not allowed to draw onto the site (it is one of the few surviving 'street fairs') before Sunday evening, so the hectic build-up can be imagined. It is acknowledged as being the best two-day fair in the country, and attracts amusements all the way from the eastern counties.

7 To Londoners the annual fairs on Hampstead Heath have always been places to visit. The skyline of the fair has changed a lot since the previous photograph. With the coming of steam, both as power for the shows and for haulage, equipment tended to be bigger and more complicated; the bulky looking Helter Skelter could be easily transported from ground to ground. The tober is decorated with flags and bunting, and market traders selling fruit and vegetables mix with the more traditional fairground attractions on Good Friday 1912. Three separate sites are used for the amusements at 'Happy Hampstead' during holiday times and the public turn up in their hundreds. Everyone in the London area associates Hampstead with fairs at holiday times, but there are others. For those living south of the Thames, those on Blackheath Common are probably the best known.

8 Country fairs have their own particular fascination. Before the coming of public transport in the form of motor buses, and when only the rich could afford a motor car, villagers used to rely heavily for diversion on the local show and fair when it visited their area. The fair was their summer entertainment and in winter there were sometimes concerts, films and magic lantern shows in the local Village Hall. This scene is Harpenden September Fair in 1890. No steam here for power—everything is horse-drawn and there are no big rides. The fair is centred around two large sets of Swings, with supporting side-stuff.

9 The village green or local meadow was the ideal setting for the village fair. This is the annual fair at Pickmere, Cheshire in the 1920s. The centrepiece is the Roundabout, while on the left are the Swings, now renamed Airships. The engine providing the power is Silcock's Burrell No 1675, *The Wonder*. An extension has been fitted to its chimney to carry the smoke away, up and over the fair. The barrel in front of the engine provides refills of water for the boiler.

10 Newcastle-upon-Tyne's fair takes place during the third week of June; it is often called the Temperance Festival. This mammoth fair — one of the largest in the country — attracts showmen from as far afield as London and even Scotland. It is held on Town Moor, only about a mile from the city centre at the side of the Great North Road. Many thousands visit this fair during its eight-day opening, but the climax comes on the closing Saturday when the horse races — the 'Pitman's Derby' — take place just across the road. Newcastle must have the largest fairground of any, as there are nearly thirty acres of land devoted to it. This is the scene of the Newcastle Hoppings at Greenwater Pool in 1914. The Helter Skelter still dominates the sky, while closer to the ground are the Joy Wheel, Gallopers and a Scenic Railway. A set of Steam Yachts is also doing good business. The edge of the fair is full of side-stuff, stalls with only the frontage open to the public. Behind the fair are the many caravans in which the showmen live and travel.

11 Tradition plays a large part in the showman's life. Many of the long established fairs had an official opening, usually with the mayor making a speech from the steps of a large ride and then touring the amusements. Mitcham Fair goes back to the 1700s; here in August 1911 the local dignitaries are seen opening the fair with a huge golden key, $4\frac{1}{2}$ft long, which is referred to as the chartered key of Mitcham, even though this one is not in fact a charter fair. The key is still in use today.

12 The Stratford-upon-Avon Mop was originally a hiring fair and still takes place on 12 October. It opens with a civic procession and there has always been a tradition of ox-roasting, a feature of many of the back-end run (autumn) fairs. This photograph was taken by Sir Benjamin Stone at Stratford in 1895. Behind the ox-roast is Tom Clarke's Switchback and Burrell showman's engine No 1820 *Victoria*, new in 1895. The ox-roast is still part of the Stratford Mop Fairs.

13 Street fairs are the result of long traditions. The annual street fair in Pinner for example goes back to 1336, when it was granted a charter. Here in 1936 the fair is back in town with a set of Gallopers dominating the foreground, sandwiched between a telephone box and the sign of the Red Lion pub. The traffic jams resulting from these street fairs can be imagined. In recent years the police have tended to seal off the street fairs and divert the traffic around them.

14 Many favourite fairgrounds are situated on low lying meadows, near rivers or streams. Before radio became commonplace, there were no weather forecasts for showmen to tune in to and so they had to rely on their own weather knowledge. Such riverside locations were prone to flooding and a sudden cloudburst could bring catastrophe. This photograph is of James Cole's Gondolas caught in the floods at Maidenhead in 1926. The showman has started to dismantle the ride, but has been caught by the rising waters. One of the rides to suffer most from such conditions was the Gallopers; if the owners did not have time to dismantle the platforms, the water would float them upwards, so breaking the legs off the horses.

12

20

21

24

26 Farrar's Scenic Whales was fitted with a very large 112-key Gaudin Organ. The organ with its show front takes up the entire width of the centre of the ride. The size of the organ and the carved whales on the cars can be judged by comparison with the size of the figures in the foreground. This set of whales was later destroyed by fire. Part of the very finely painted top rounding boards can be seen above the pillars. This photograph was possibly taken just after World War I.

27 The Chairoplane is another ride to be based on a revolving centre. Here the platform remains stationary and the riders are carried in chairs suspended by chains from the revolving top. In full flight, a set of chairs is an exciting ride to see, with the riders swinging far out over the watching public. This German-built set is seen at Drypool Green Fair, Hull, in 1925. The rounding boards are lettered 'American Swing Swing', and it seats a total of thirty-six patrons. Several of these electrically driven rides came over from Germany in 1923, proving popular with the patrons and riding masters alike. The latter approved of them because they required few workmen and only one engine. This ride had been brought to Drypool Green from Girlington on the outskirts of Bradford by a 1905 Fowler Engine, No 10318 *Sunny Boy No 2*. This journey had been accomplished in record time thanks to the solid rubber tyres just fitted to the engine. These became compulsory by law in 1926. The van on the right-hand side is a particularly fine example of a small showman's living van, being only twelve feet in length.

28 The first Cakewalk to visit Nottingham Goose Fair was this example in 1909 belonging to A. Richards of Hull; it had come directly from Fun City at Olympia, London. This was a ride consisting of a number of oscillating platforms on which the patrons were challenged to stay upright as they walked through it. Its name is derived from a Negro dance. Some showmen paid dancers to ride it for hours on end to attract other customers. On the left is an adaptation of the Foden steam wagon, Number 7141, for showmen's use. The wagon has the traditional twisted brass and a dynamo mounted on the front end of the boiler which provides the power for the ride. The larger-than-usual crowd around the Cakewalk is due to the presence of the Mayoral party which had just opened the 1909 fair, and were having a ride on the machine. Behind and to the left, can be seen the front of Bostock & Wombwell's Menagerie.

29

30

29 Nowadays visitors to a traction engine rally or similar event are quite accustomed to seeing many different types of fairground organ in preservation. Usually they are presented by their owners from the backs of motor lorries or trailers, as this is the easiest way for them to be transported. In the heyday of the fair, these great mechanical instruments featured at the front of the shows or in the centre of the rides. The idea, quite simply, was to attract the flattie (fairground patron) to the show. Showmen vied with each other to have the most highly decorated organ, or preferably the loudest! They were often badly out of tune, very much in the way that records amplified over the average fairground speaker to day are almost unrecognisable. On smaller fairs however, there were often no big rides, so the showman might have just one big organ strategically placed to attract visitors to the fair itself. One such was used by Arnold Brothers in the south of England, seen here in 1931. In the 1930s when there was widespread trade depression, a lot of showmen replaced organs with a loud-speaker system or panatrope so as to keep in business. The big organs were operated by using books of cardboard 'music'; they needed a permanent attendant, and it also meant another load on the road. So the panatropes, which were worked from a turntable in the roundabout's paybox and used cheap gramophone records, saved a man's wage and an extra load.

30 It is unusual to find a period photograph of an organ away from its ride or show. Here we see the large Military Band Organ owned by the West Country firm of Anderton and Rowland at the works of Orton and Spooner where its show front was designed and fitted in 1906. This 98-key Marenghi organ was first of all fitted into a Bioscope Show. Later, when such shows went out of fashion, it was cut down and put into a scenic ride. The organ is still owned by the De Vey family (née Anderton) and is regularly shown at traction engine rallies.

31 One of the tallest rides at any fair is the Big Wheel, sometimes known as the Eli Wheel or Ferris Wheel. Versions of this have been known for many years, but with the coming of steam bigger and better wheels could be produced, as well as ones which revolved faster. This picture was taken at an Oxford Fair in 1895 and clearly shows the stationary steam engine which was used to drive the wheel.

32

33

32   The Dodgem track was first patented in 1921, but it had been preceded by the Brooklands Speedway, an oval track around which the cars raced. Usually the cars were electrically driven but in this case small petrol engines are used. In practice these were not as reliable as the electric variety. This set is by Supercar of Leamington Spa, and was photographed at King's Lynn in 1939. The fairground organ for drawing crowds to the ride has been superseded by the panatrope, a loudspeaker mounted on the top of the central paybox and playing popular music from records.

33   The most common version of the Dodgem or Bumper Car was this type, powered by electricity collected from the overhead wire mesh. Dodgem tracks were usually fully covered and brightly lit. This picture was taken at the May Day Fair at Knutsford Heath in 1936. The Dodgems is a ride which has stood the test of time, and is still a firm favourite. In the early days the cars gave a lot of trouble, and it was possible to see more out of action than those in actual use. Large tracks were frowned upon by showmen, as they discovered that cars reached a much higher speed, and damage from bumping was much greater. As with motor cars, body design has altered. When television came into general use, it cost Dodgem owners quite a lot to fit suppressors to their fleets. If house holders suffered ruined picture reception they would take steps to abolish the fair!

34   One of the new machines to come out of the 1930s was the Moon Rocket. Charles Openshaw of Reading patented the idea in 1936, and it is illustrated here in one of its simplest forms. The thrill of the ride is obtained from the speed at which the cars travel and the centrifugal force created by use of a slope. This is a German-made machine at a Newcastle-upon-Tyne Fair in 1938, owned by the showman John Collins. Many Moon Rockets are far more ornate than this one with elaborate top rounding boards; some had a counter-rotating centre to heighten the effect. Moon Rockets were built in Britain by R. J. Lakin of Streatham.

35 One of the simplest forms of ride was the Swing, a slightly more complicated version of the childrens swings found in parks or playgrounds. In fact this ride was often called a Park Swing. Usually it consisted of a boat carrying two or more people, who pulled on overhead ropes to set it in motion. A later version shown here is known as Over the Tops, Looping the Loop, or Bird Cages. The circular cage always remained horizontal, and the efforts of the caged patrons provided the action. It was every rider's aim to get the cage to go over the top. This is a set owned by Arnold Brothers just before the last war. Note the prominently placed loudspeaker.

36 The Helter Skelter is one of the oldest features of the fairground; sometimes it is called the Lighthouse Slip, now often shortened to purely 'Slip'. It has the advantage of having no mechanical components, the participants sliding down the spiral chute by gravity. Here the Slip dominates South Shields Market Square around the turn of the century. Like the Big Wheel, the Slip is often used as a beacon to attract punters to the fair at night, but this photograph was taken before electricity was widely used for this purpose. At this time, however, the ride would have been illuminated at night with the aid of naptha flare lamps, the traditional lighting of the fairground and the market. One such lamp, for example, would have been hung on the pole which can be seen at the top of the Slip at right angles to it.

The Slip was a difficult amusement to build, and was vulnerable to strong winds, but once erected, it gave trouble-free operation. The proprietor usually sat in a paybox at the top of the lower staircase; the rider was given a mat to sit on and then climbed the stairs and slid down. There was a man at the bottom to assist; he also stacked the mats in a neat pile for future patrons. There are some modern Slips of lattice-work construction, much smaller and better suited to windy conditions.

37 An unusual view of a Helter Skelter taken from the top looking down on two fairgoers descending in tandem. At the bottom a crowd has collected to watch the antics of those finishing the trip. Those in the know slow themselves down before they reach the bottom—otherwise they tend to shoot straight off the finishing pad into the crowd. One modification to the Slip was the Bowl Slide which finished with the patrons circling a bowl at the end of the trip. Much amusement was caused by their efforts to climb out.

38 One of the most exciting rides ever to be presented on the fairground were the Steam Yachts. They were a development of a steam swing produced by Henry Cracknell and William Cartwright in the late 1880s. Savages of King's Lynn built two sets in 1894, and it was their version which became known as the Yachts. The drive came from a portable steam engine in the centre and was connected to the two boats by a chain; the steam engine is behind the organ in the centre under the awning. Baker's Steam Yachts are seen here at a Newcastle fair in June, 1914; on this occasion they were riding at 1d all classes. The boats were named *Lusitania* and *Mauretania*.

4

39 A much earlier version of Over the Tops was this Overboat, which was in a way a very small Big Wheel. The highly ornate boats were suspended within a square frame which in turn was operated from a central point. Some were hand cranked, others worked by steam and later by electricity. The patrons would often swing the boat as well. This is a rare set of two—a double set of Overboats. In order to maintain balance (to even out the load) it was frequently necessary to add heavy weights in one of the cars, particularly on hand-operated sets. This pre-World War I scene is in the London area, probably on Hampstead Heath.

40 Some riding masters in the North of England got together in the late 1920s to form the Palm Beach Amusement Company. One of the rides they travelled was a Figure of Eight, a smaller version of the Big Dipper, a ride more usually associated with permanent amusement parks, often at the seaside. The Figure of Eight was only suitable for really big fairs since building up took a considerable time and required extra workmen. In relation to the distance travelled by the patron, this is a very compact and thrilling ride, but operating costs prevented it from enjoying great popularity amongst the showmen. In this view can be seen a truck lettered 'John Murphy's Proud Peacocks'. This is one of the scenery trucks with low arched roofs, which made them suitable for rail transit as they came within the limits of the loading gauge.

41 A ride for the young or those trying to show off to their friends, the Joy Wheel had only limited popularity with the travelling showman. The idea was for the patrons to try and stay on a rapidly revolving disc, which often had a conical centre. This is Collins' Joy Wheel at Nottingham Goose Fair in 1910. The price of admission included the facility to watch or ride as you wished. The Joy Wheel did not last very long, as it was not suited to all members of the family. In the 1920s an attempt was made to revive the Joy Wheel with a 'miniature edition' in the form of the Devil's Disc, but it too was short-lived and very few were built. They were the type of ride the showman called a 'oncer'—as few people would come back for a second try.

42 The Devil's Disc was a spinning ride, enclosed on three sides; the fronts often had incredible painted decor such as this. Here the fairground decorator has really been able to let rip, and the result must have been thought very daring for the period, the 1920s. The fairground workers posing amongst the frolics are completely dwarfed by the monstrous and almost obscene characterisation of life in Hell.

43 As the taste of the general public began to change, showmen modified the style of painting on their rides. This is Farrars' Super Speedway. Gone is the Victorian style of decoration—a much more modern type has taken its place. This ride would not look out of place in a fair today. The paintwork would last many years if it was carefully looked after and would be regularly scrubbed, touched up and varnished. Each item would be separately packed away to avoid scratching and chafing. Note the hundreds of electric light bulbs on this ride.

The Shows

HULL FAIR
1919

44 In the early years of the century, it was the shows which were the major attractions at fairs. The public rarely ventured far from home in those days and relied on entertainments being brought to them. One very popular crowd puller was what was then called 'The Wild Beasts Show', and there were several of them. Most of the people had their first glimpse of such animals at the travelling menagerie, since permanent zoos were practically unknown. Best known of this kind of show was Bostock & Wombwell's Menagerie which travelled throughout the British Isles, showing on its own, but always attended the October fairs at Nottingham and Hull. A band played on the front as an inducement to patrons. It often showed for one-day stands in the smaller towns and villages. As early as 1840 Wombwell had no less than twenty-nine different animals travelling, including twelve lions, eight tigers, three elephants and three giraffes. This scene is at Hull at the eight-day fair in 1919. The large crowd is typical of the period, and the pelican is also being used as a front-of-the-house attraction.

46 Pat Collins' Bioscope Show was one of the largest travelling. It was decorated by 5,600 coloured lights, and featured in the centre a magnificent 98-key Marenghi Organ. This great organ has been preserved, and is now owned by Bill Hunt of Oldbury. One of the traction engines which supplied the power can be seen on the extreme right. At one time, Pat Collins travelled four big shows, and needed as many as twenty-five traction engines to transport them. Later he opened a chain of permanent cinemas in the Midlands.

5   Moving pictures, as the early films were known, came into being before the turn of the century and showman Randall Williams introduced them to the fairground in 1896, claiming them to be the greatest scientific invention of the age. In view of their immense popularity, many other showmen concentrated on this new form of entertainment, and they were known on the fairs as Bioscope Shows. Permanent cinemas came into being before World War I, and thus ended the days of the Bioscope on the fairgrounds. In the south, however, Arnold Brothers ran their Bioscope Show up until 1922, when it was sold, and in the middle 1920s Bingo Cinema used to appear in a few Scottish villages. The superb frontage of Jacob Studt's Bioscope is typical of many. There is a mechanical organ on one side of the entrance with possibly as many as 110 keys, and a traction engine on the other. It is interesting to see how the carved work has been adapted to fit on to the traction engine's awning, as it stands in front of the show. Such shows were brilliantly illuminated, in this case with twenty-two arc lights. In the centre is a royal coat of arms to show that the Bioscope had been attended by royalty. Behind the frontage was a simple rectangular tent which could accommodate up to 1,000 people in which the films were shown.

47 A fair such as Oxford St Giles would have many different types of show. Here in 1885 two differing ones were built up alongside; on the left is Lawrence's Anglo-American Marionettes, an extraordinary puppet show, while on the right Chittock has performing dogs and monkeys. The marionette show is in progress, and Chittock has started his front-of-the-house show to draw in the next batch of patrons. The crowds are being entertained by a drummer and trumpeter accompanying the barrel organ, plus a few of the performing monkeys. The barker or spieler has yet to make his announcements. Each show vied with the other for custom, so prices had to be competitive. Admission to Chittock's was 3d.

As horses were used for moving the loads from one fairground to another, the rolling stock had to be limited in size and weight. Each show was made up of a number of different wagons: the wheels of some of these can be seen underneath the frontage of Lawrence's marionettes.

48 With the coming of the cinematograph, films were often incorporated in beast shows. A screen could be lowered on rollers in front of a cage of lions for example, the animals keeping up a continuous roar throughout the silent film. Here at Torquay Regatta Fair about 1900 the front-on-the-house show is on at Hancock's Palace, with two children boxing. On the left is the showman's engine while on the right can be seen a large organ. Jones's Circus Varieties on the right was an adaptation of the traditional circus to the fairground sideshow.

49 and **50** Serious theatre was at
one time part of the fairground
scene, when bands of travelling
actors would set up amongst the
other sideshows. If the people were
unable to get to the theatre, then the
theatre came to the people. They
used the same attractions on the
front as other shows, the organ for
example, as well as actors
who played a small part of the show free
to the waiting crowds. This is
Holloway's show at Birmingham,
June 1903. One wonders how many
of the old music halls, variety
theatres and cinemas took their
names from the shows on the
fairgrounds.

51 and **52** Before television
provided mass entertainment, there
were numerous theatres showing
variety. Many people preferred a
'live' show to pictures. When the
variety show opened, there was
usually some spectacular dancing by
the chorus girls, and the 'high
steppers' added a touch of glamour.
On the fairgrounds the paraders
danced on the show front to tunes
played on the organ, and they
certainly attracted the crowds. The
outside show was entirely free.
Top, the can-can girls performing
out front at Stratford-upon-Avon
Mop Fair in 1908. *Below*, the more
modern equivalent at Mitcham Fair
limbering up behind the scenes
before appearing out front.

53 The coming of the Cinematograph and the Bioscope Shows rendered the more traditional theatre shows obsolete. Mammy Paine's Coliseum changed from theatre to acts of mystery and conjuring. At the same time, they announced on large notices outside that theirs was not a picture show, it was real live entertainment. It is interesting to see that here, in the early 1920s, at Newcastle-upon-Tyne, virtually every member of the crowd is wearing a hat!

54 Front-of-the-house attractions were not confined to dancing girls. The menagerie shows used to display some of their animals. In the case of Bostock & Wombwell's Menagerie, Billy the pelican was a favourite for many years. Here he is seen at a Nottingham Goose Fair, probably after World War I. Wearing all the medals is the star of the show—Captain Fred Wombwell—who must surely be the most famous wild animal trainer of all time. To see him enter the lions' cage and put the animals through their paces was an unforgettable sight. While the lions growled and snarled, Captain Wombwell would shout orders in a voice like thunder. Backstage, however, the Captain was very quietly spoken, and a more affectionate couple than he and his wife would be difficult to find. But performing with wild animals in such a restricted space as a 'beast van' called for great agility; rheumatism forced the Captain to relinquish his position as ace performer during the menagerie's last few years on the road. It was then when Captain Wombwell set up a stall in the menagerie where, for a few copper coins, the youngsters could buy apples, buns, etc, for feeding the animals. No scales were used—it was a 'handful' a time, so the wise ones always bought from the Captain, as he had the biggest hand! The placards on the front of the show read 'Grander and better than ever for this visit', 'See the Wilde Beaste or horned horse', 'See the baby tigers, the first ever born with a travelling menagerie', 'See the almost human apes'.

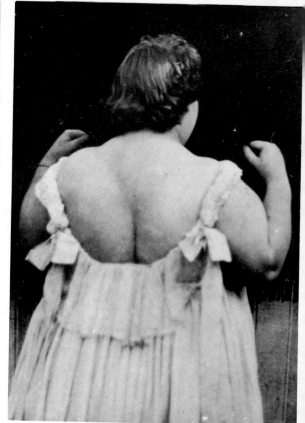

5 Many years ago sports were part of the fair, particularly in country areas. As the fairs grew up, boxing and wrestling became part of the established travelling scene. Even in the television age, the few remaining boxing and wrestling booths are still popular and some wellknown champions have come from the booths. It was a tough life on the booths; on one occasion at the Durham Miners' Gala of 1919, Billy Wood of Dumfries fought eighteen fights in one day, stopping fifteen of his opponents within the distance, and the miners could be very tough. Some would travel to five different fairs in eight days, fighting some eight times a day, as well as pulling down the booth, travelling to the next venue and building up again. This is Oxford St Giles Fair in 1898 and it is interesting to see that the proprietor is trying to attract the ladies as well as the gentlemen.

56 and **57** Freak Shows have always been a popular line with showmen. Some were live shows, others used stuffed animals. All manner of animal freaks have been shown, but it is the human element which really attracts the customers. Nowadays they are mainly dwarfs, giants, very thin or very fat people. There are a few tattooed ladies, but people are too sensitive to pay money to see people with deformities. Beautiful Marie was a fat lady, but as here in the 1900s she was young, she was billed as a giant schoolgirl. Outside the booth the showman uses a trumpet barrel organ to draw in the crowds while inside Marie does not seem to be quite as fat as the artist's drawing. Shows presenting animal freaks are under fire these days, as there are frequent objections by 'animal lovers'.

58 Mary Ann Bevan had a sad life; she left home at an early age and went to work on a Kent farm. She married and had four children, and her husband was killed in World War I. She developed an incurable disease which affected her facial characteristics, as well as enlarging her hands and feet. One day she read about a competition with a £100 prize to find the ugliest woman in the world; she entered and won. She later travelled widely with the fairs and died at the age of 45. On the Mary Ann Bevan show can be seen two brass bells. These were popular with those presenting shows, and much more effective than the loud hailers of today.

59 The coming of the microphone and loudspeaker made the spieler's job much easier, as can be seen at Norwich Fair in 1937. The half man, half woman was a common form of sideshow at one time; with careful training it was possible for a person to develop muscles and other characteristics on one side of the body only. This one is competing with a girlie show. Oriental mysteries are now a thing of the past, since they are not daring enough for the modern fairgoer; strip shows have taken their place. Long established showmen have a very high sense of morality; to them the strip show is anathema.

60 Fortune tellers have been part of the fairground scene from the earliest days. Nowadays they operate out of expensive caravans, but for many years they used small tents which they carried around with them, often on foot. Phillip Allingham in his book *Cheapjack* describes his first fortune telling booth: 'I was getting short of cash, but I bought a garden shelter at Gamage's for thirty-five shillings. I also purchased an incense-holder, some incense, and a number of eastern trays from Woolworths, and when I had draped some cloth across the open front of my shelter it made a pretty good fortune telling booth.' There could be as many as one hundred fortune tellers at a big fair such as Hull. The small tents used by what were known as 'tick offs' had one big disadvantage to the palmist: when the fair was closed they were the obvious choice for a toilet.

61 Thomas Burke took this photograph of a Liverpool fair in 1895. Throwing games have always been one of the most popular sideshows, often called Aunt Sally Shows. 'Three balls a penny' used to be the charge. By the expression on this lady's face, trade must have been very bad indeed though it must be admitted that there is very little to attract the public to this stall.

62 One tends to think of the Coconut Shy as a sideshow of long standing. However during the 1800s coconuts were an expensive fruit and the earliest form of this game was for the punter to hurl large sticks at baskets balance on poles at the back of the booth. Many of the stalls retain the red sheets with white lettering of the type seen before World War I. Here trade looks busy on the Coconut Shy at Hampstead Heath in June 1922.

63 Games involving shooting at targets with rifles have always had a high popularity, even where showmen give no prizes to the successful. This is a small and neat travelling shooting gallery, seen on Hampstead Heath in 1898, where the customers are trying to shoot the bowls off clay pipes. This particular show is mounted on a hand barrow to keep weight down. There is very little protection behind the stall to catch stray shots, and no sides to contain ricochets. Stalls such as this would not be tolerated at a modern fair because of the lack of safety precautions.

64 and **65**   Though there is only one Wall of Death currently travelling in this country, it still pulls in packed houses wherever it goes. Traditionally the building is shaped like a farm silo with the riders performing on the inside and the public viewing the show from a gallery at the top. The most usual form of Wall features motorcycle riders giving exhibitions of all sorts of trick riding on the vertical sides of the wooden drome. Tommy Messham nowadays includes a

bicycle rider as a contrast! The idea of using midget cars came from the United States in the 1920s, and in order to give greater thrills lions as sidecar passengers were quite extensively used. Barry's Sensational Motordrome *(top)* pictured at a Norwich Fair in 1939 was one of the last to use this trick. The driver carrying a lion as passenger *(below)* is the American lion tamer Mr Egbert who was performing at a Mitcham fair in the 1930s.

66 A simpler version of the Wall of Death was the Globe of Death. Here in 1922 the riders performed inside a globe with slatted sides which allowed the visitors to view it from outside, so eliminating a great deal of structure to be carried about and erected. An even simpler version of the Globe has appeared as an act in theatres; this was known as the Saucer, since only the top part of the globe was used. As a finale the Saucer would be lifted to the top of the stage with a rider circling in it. The motorcycles used in these shows were usually highly modified versions of large-capacity American machines such as Indians or Harley Davidsons. Often the frame would be shortened, the forks reinforced and extra leaves added to the springs. The handlebars would be altered, and all road equipment removed. The riders were responsible for the preparation of their own machines; any mechanical fault which developed when they were travelling at up to 45mph could have been fatal.

67 Showmen play heavily on the ego. Get a crowd around a Striker and he can drum up any number of customers to have a go. In theory, the harder you hit the base of the Striker the further the market goes up the pole, and if you are lucky it will ring the bell. No prizes here, you do it just for the honour and glory. Get a group of young men and their girls, and their desire to show off will keep the money rolling in. This is Hampstead Heath in 1930, with two girls obviously posing for the press photographer. A few Strikers have survived. At one time there were juvenile Strikers and the child always got a prize of some sort, determined by where the indicator stopped.

68 Arcades of slot machines are very numerous at fairs today, but they were late arrivals on the fairgrounds. One of the first to introduce them was Birmingham showman Joe Fletcher, in the early 1920s. They were not too popular with showmen as many local by-laws forbade 'games of chance', and the police were very active in stopping their appearance in such areas. Many types of slot machines were to be found; the seaside 'What the Butler Saw' or the ones which told your fortune were the most common. Others produced an X-ray picture of the patron or even a picture of his mother-in-law! There were many ball games, such as this football one, where you paid 2d and the winner received 1d back.

Popular with the teenagers was the Punchball Machine and 'Test Your Grips' which showed on a clock dial the number of pounds you could grip. A version of the latter had an electric coil and dry battery, and by gripping and turning the handle, you could increase the electric shock given; a dial showing you the amount of shock you could take.

69 Showmen have a tradition of being a God-fearing race. Many of the mighty organs had a large repertoire of hymn tunes and other religious music. The Oxford Bible Stall is an example of a religious group taking their beliefs to the people at Oxford St Giles Fair in 1880. Around this time, however, there would normally be no fairs or Bioscope Shows on Sundays. The late Mrs Arnold is reputed to have told the story that when, for the first time, Arnold Brothers opened their Bioscope Show on a Sunday (in Somerset in 1908), disaster struck soon afterwards. There was a very bad storm that evening which blew down half the show. It was regarded by locals and fairground folk as retribution for opening on the Lord's Day. In later years when Sunday opening became more commonplace, there was often a religious service conducted from the steps of the Gallopers before the fair opened. Religious groups are still to be seen at the really big fairs, such as Newcastle, Hull and Nottingham.

70 A traditional part of the fair from the middle ages onwards was the hawker who, with very little equipment, attended the gatherings selling whatever he could lay his hands on. The coming of compulsory licences for such traders has reduced their numbers drastically. In 1911 this hawker in Nottingham is selling tickling sticks, monkeys on a stick, bags of confetti, balls on a piece of elastic, and many strings of beads. Also on sale would have been 'ladies' tormentors', a lead tube around $3\frac{1}{2}$in long filled with water. The water would be squirted onto girls attending the fair and then the poor unfortunate lady would be showered with confetti. Sometimes showmen would apparently take pity on girls who had been covered in confetti and offer to turn them upside down and shake the confetti out of their clothes. They would then collect together the fallen confetti and re-sell it! After the fair closed, they would also collect up the discarded tubes and refill them with water for sale the next day.

71 and 72 Ever since the first fairs, people have been peddling food at these gatherings. Here, at the turn of the century, we see a lemonade stall and also one selling whelks and jellied eels. Another very popular stall was the panam, which sold such items as coconuts, brandy snaps and other sweetmeats. Items such as tea and sandwiches were unobtainable in the early days. At modern fairs, of course, you will find many stalls tempting you to buy hot dogs, hamburgers, fish and chips or candyfloss.

Building Up & Pulling Down

73 To the layman, building up a fair must appear as a chaotic process. To the showman however, it is a very precise operation. The rides must be built up completely level, whatever the slope of the ground may be. Here is a view of King's Lynn market place in 1925 with the annual fair in course of erection. Recognised by showmen as the opening event of the season, King's Lynn Mart (a charter fair still held annually on the centrally located site), commences on 14 February, St Valentine's Day. Farrar Brothers are building up their Scenic Whales, the Switchback track is in position, and the centre truck (containing the organ around which will be built the scenery) has been raised up on blocks. Farrars' Fowler Engine *Reliance* can be seen on the left of the organ, and on the right is Ling's Fowler *The Great Bear*. Both belong to Doncaster-based showmen, evidence of the importance of this fair to amusement caterers. The gigantic whales in which the patrons will ride on the Scenic Railway are sheeted in the foreground. On the right-hand side of the picture is an engine sheeted over, probably one of Thurston's Burrells.

74 Building up at Barnet Fair in 1919. The Helter Skelter on the left is being built up from within, and the chutes around the side will be put on last of all. The Gallopers still have to have their horses fixed to the poles; after this the floor of the ride will be built up. The Scenic and Joy Wheel have apparently been completed. The painting on the Slip is made to resemble the stonework of a lighthouse. Fitting the outside 'chutes' started at the bottom, and sections were carried up them singly until the top was reached. This was not easy, for anyone holding one of those heavy chutes (a two-handed job) was apt to slip, and then slide right down to the bottom.

75 On many sites it was difficult for showmen to build up on flat land. Here at Chipping Norton Mop Fair they have been given a very tricky site to work, on a distinct slope. Nowadays this would not be tolerated. When building up, much packing material would be needed under the ride to even it up and it was virtually impossible for a patron to mount the ride on the far side. Ideally, a riding master would wish his patrons to be evenly spread around his machine, so taking the strain off the mechanism. In this situation it is obviously an impossibility unless he is riding full. To stop patrons all climbing on at once, the driver would never quite stop the ride. The showman's engine in the background is an Aveling and Porter; the photograph was taken around 1920.

76 While most of the work of setting up a fair has to be manual, mechanisation has been applied in some instances. Here a Scenic Railway is being built up; the centre and the organ are in position and so is the track. The heaviest item is however, the set of cars in which the patrons ride. These are being lifted onto the track by a crane fixed to the bunker of a scenic showman's engine. These cranes were capable of lifting some 30cwt; the winch on the engine provides the lift. This picture was taken at Barnet Fair in September, 1923. Car-lift cranes were introduced about 1918, as the brainwave of Bradford showman Goldthorpe Marshall. In view of their immediate success they subsequently became standard equipment on all engines of scenic type. The steel wire rope fitted to the engines came in useful for this extra duty.

77 Preparations are in hand for the opening of the fair at Barnet around 1915. The cars on Abbott and Barker's Scenic Railway have been uncovered and the round stall on the right is ready for business. In this instance, the showman's engine was only providing power for the lights which were not required until dusk, so it is still sheeted and the fire unlit. The Scenic Railway has its own centre engine to provide the motion. Note the beautiful pillars on the ride; they would have been skilfully painted to give a marbled effect. The extreme height of these pillars is unusual. The round stall on the right is a version of the Hoopla 'rings and blocks'. The table is covered by a lovely velvet cloth which would have been decorated with gold embroidery and golden tassels.

78 Fairground rides are always highly decorated, with many parts. When a showman has two or even three fairs to cover in a week, he must be sure his loads are packed carefully to avoid damage. Pieces must always be put back into the packing truck in just the right order for getting them out again. Often they are numbered to facilitate this process. Here, at Hampstead Heath in 1932, Harry Gray's Ark is being packed up. There had been a storm deluge the previous day and the ground is like a quagmire. Most packing trucks are fitted with front or side belly boxes under the main platform to provide extra storage space. In horse-drawn days, these were usually at the front or the back, as the large wheels would have precluded the fitting of any at the side. A front belly box is clearly shown in this photograph. The story is told of a fairground worker and his wife who slept for ten years in one of these front belly boxes.

79 It usually takes a full day to build up a large ride, but it can be done more quickly should the need arise, and if there are enough staff. They come down more quickly; often a fair would pull down on a Saturday night, move on to a new ground overnight, build up on Sunday, and open again on Monday. Nottingham Goose Fair, for example, closes just before midnight on the Saturday, and many of the showmen are open again at Hull for 11 o'clock on the Monday morning. Here at Mitcham in 1936 a gaff worker is taking a Juvenile Galloper horse and cockerel to the packing truck. When a fair is being built up, usually the big machines are dealt with first; then the juveniles and side-stuff are built around them. The reverse procedure is adopted when pulling down. Hence in this case the Juvenile is being dismantled, while the Chairoplanes remain built up in the background. The chairs have been tied up to prevent any of the children from trying to swing on them!

80 After the fair is over . . . . Many of the big rides have already been dismantled and moved on, leaving behind a rearguard of workers to clear up the fairground here at Hampstead in the 1930s. In some cases there was not enough transport available to take all the loads in one go, so the living vans were left and the engines returned for them later. It was imperative that the fairground should be left clean and tidy after the fair had moved on, otherwise there was a good chance that the showmen would not be allowed back the following year.

Power on the Road & for the Rides

81 Moving a fair on the road has always been a complicated business. In horse-drawn days of course loads were limited, though it was not unusual to see as many as six horses pulling trucks from some of the larger shows. Because the loads had to be broken down into smaller units there were more of them. There is in existence a photograph of Sedgwick's Menagerie halted between fairs which shows thirteen horse-drawn trucks. This photograph is of Bostock & Wombwell's Menagerie on the move in 1913. The vans used for accommodating wild animals obviously had to be of exceptional strength; they were, therefore, of enormous weight too.

82 The Menageries were at a slight advantage when it came to transport as they could harness one or two of their animals; in this case an elephant is pulling the load at the Newcastle-upon-Tyne in 1913. Certain more docile animals could also be hitched on behind, so saving another wheeled vehicle. At one Nottingham Goose Fair held on the Forest site, heavy rain had turned the Tober into a morass and the traction engines were bogged down when it came to leaving, but a travelling zoo scored by having the elephant to assist in rescue work. Before the advent of the Showman's Guild and better organisation, it was a case of first come first served at any new ground. Hence the dash from one venue to another was often hectic. Lord George Sanger tells of a battle between Hilton and Wombwell's Menagerie on the Reading to Henley Road. The Wombwell drivers tried to overtake the others in their efforts to get to Henley in time to secure the best places. Caravans were overturned, beast wagons broken open and the animals allowed to escape. Sanger writes: 'We had a good day after all for business, though it was the sorriest lot of battered performers and damaged caravans that Henley Fair had ever witnessed.'

84 With a full head of steam, T. Smith and Sons' Foden Showman's Engine No 528 is winched away from Victoria Park Fairground, Hayward's Heath, Sussex, in August 1939, after becoming bogged in the muddy ground. The engine is fitted with rubbers on the wheels; all the caravans have small wheels with pneumatic tyres which made for easier running on the roads and higher overall speeds. The two engines doing the winching are Tasker tractors No 1770 and 1675.

83 With the coming of the steam traction engine, showmen quickly adapted it for their purposes. One of these was to pull the loads from one fairground to another. Gone were the single trucks pulled by horses; in their stead came the long road train, with its engines hauling as many as ten trailers with a total weight of fifty tons or more. In early times the showman adapted his horse-drawn trucks to the new motive power, hence the long loads. Later came legislation restricting the number of trailers, so special packing trucks were evolved to carry heavier individual loads. Here, around 1910, we see Chipperfield's Electric Theatre, one of the large Bioscope Shows, on the road, drawn by Burrell Showman's Engine No 2281, *Queen of the Midlands.* This engine was built in 1900.

85 On this occasion a defect in the steering mechanism on Burrell No 2803 has made Sangers hastily add shafts and a horse to assist with the steering, or was it a well thought out gimmick to attract the photographers from the local paper? The scene was Torquay, about 1922. The peculiar 'hairnet' over the chimney of the engine is a spark arrester; engines not so fitted have been known to set fire to thatched cottages or corn-fields. In recent years one even started a fire in the grass surrounding an army ammunition dump, to the consternation of the authorities.

86 Before the coming of the steam traction engine, fairground loads were all horse-drawn. Then it was often quicker when moving from one fairground to another, some distance away, to take the loads by rail. The coming of the traction engine did not always change this procedure, for provided that all arrangements were made in advance, it would still be quicker than travelling by road, particularly before rubber tyres on the engines became compulsory. What was tedious, however, was the transportation of the vehicles to the railway station, loading them one by

one at the dock, and reversing the procedure at the other end. For example, when Hull Fair began almost immediately after closing day at Nottingham, the LNE and LMS Railways vied with each other in running special trains for fairground tackle.

W. H. Marshall & Sons used to have a fleet of four big traction engines, and their travelling season started with the Spring Fair at Halifax, a fortnight before Easter. Here we see their Fowler No 10318 at Pellon goods yard; the engine is removing a load of the Hey-Day brought by rail from a Lancashire town; surprisingly this photograph was taken as late as 1936. Virtually no fairs travelled by rail after the last war, but some circuses continued the practice into the 1950s. The cost of moving a load by rail was as little as 6d per mile in 1908. Those travellers accompanying the load had to buy an ordinary rail ticket. Therefore the children were sometimes locked into the living van and instructed to 'keep quiet' for the length of the journey, in the hope that they would not be spotted by the railway authorities. One family is known to have travelled from Gloucester to Eastleigh in this way.

87 Not every traveller could afford one of the large showman's engines; indeed in the early days it was not necessary for him to have one as his rides might well lack electric drive. He did, however, want something to replace horses and take his ride from fair to fair. Some showmen therefore bought steam tractors which they adapted to their requirements. In this case, the Smarts had fitted a full-length cab to a Burrell general purpose road locomotive, but neither a dynamo nor twisted brass columns. They had had the canopy decorated with their name, in gold-leaf lettering. This engine is also fitted with two candle-type carriage lamps at the front. As a matter of interest, the chain from the cab upright is attached to the clothes line!

MESSRS. HANCOCK'S TRACTION ENGINE WITH ITS A

MESSRS. G. TWIGDON & SON'S TRACTION ENGINE *en route* HAULING NINE VANS AND OVER FORTY TONS.

JACOB STUDT'S STEAM CIRCUS *en route*.

88 This is a double-page spread from the 1909 catalogue of Charles Burrell and Sons of Thetford. All the vehicles which are being towed by the traction engines were formerly horse-drawn, which emphasises the great change which took place when steam haulage became regular practice. Though the catalogue illustrates a full showman's engine, it is interesting to see that none of the engines in these photographs are equipped with dynamos, as they are only being used for haulage purposes.

89 and **90** Savages built two unusual engines in 1897 and 1898 which were known as traction centres. Here was an attempt to use the same engine for haulage as well as driving the ride—mechanically as opposed to electrically. The drive was taken by vertical gearing through the cab roof to the centre of the ride. They were not a great success. One of these engines, No 728 *Enterprise,* was delivered to George Baker of Southampton to drive his set of Gallopers. Prior to this, Baker had taken delivery of engine No 1934 from Burrells of Thetford and had it converted in his own workshop to a traction centre. Possibly one was to act as a spare engine in case of breakdown. It is unlikely that the dynamo could be used at the same time as the vertical drive. This highly ornate decoration was typical of the period and very appropriate on the traction centre as it would have formed part of the ride's centre decoration. Here we see the Burrell as built in 1896 and about 1910-11, some time after conversion.

91 The steam centre-engine was for many years the main motive power for various versions of the Roundabout. Another adaptation of it, however, was to drive the Steam Yacht. Most Steam Yachts were twin-boat sets and had to be worked separately from the one boiler, so the boiler had to operate the engines on top of it. Each boat could accommodate 20-30 people; to start the boat it had to be rocked, gently at first, and gradually more and more. To do this the engine was run first one way and then reversed until sufficient momentum was gained to make it work automatically thereafter. This is Savage's Steam Yacht Centre Engine No 883, new in 1921.

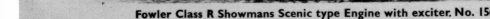

Fowler Class R Showmans Scenic type Engine with exciter. No. 15658

92 This is an illustration from a catalogue of John Fowler and Co of Leeds, showing one of their famous showman's scenic engines. 'Scenic' refers to the type of ride that such engine would accompany. Such rides have rise and fall platforms and an extra load is placed on the engine's dynamo when starting the ride with the cars on one of the uphill sections. An ordinary dynamo would throw its driving belt if suddenly subjected to this type of load, so Fowler inserted an exciter on the field side of the dynamo, to boost the power when starting. As this exciter was mounted on top of the boiler, the whole of the engine had to be lengthened.

93 Wallis and Steevens of Basingstoke made only a few showmen's engines, but in 1903 they built this 8 NHP engine for Henry Jennings of Devizes. Jennings gave it the name *Royal John*. It was fitted with a Dickinson dynamo, a make popular with showmen in the earlier days of steam. The extension chimney is in position to carry the smoke away high above the fair. The ornate paintwork is unusual on an engine.

94 A traction engine requires daily maintenance. Many parts require oiling, and the firebox needs cleaning out before the new fire is lit. There are the brasses to be cleaned and the other metal work to be kept shiny. To the riding master, his engine was part of the show, and if he was proud of his ride, he was also proud of his engine and kept it spotlessly clean. After every hundred hours of running, the boiler had to be washed out to remove rust and silt. This was often done on a Sunday when the fair was not on the move. This Burrell belonged to the St Austell-based firm of J. Rowland and is believed to be No 3660 *Victor*, built in 1915 and scrapped in 1950, seen here in the 1930s.

95 The showman's engines which provided the power were often situated within the fair itself so that the drivers could see the person in charge of the machine, and thus know when maximum load was required. This also allowed much shorter lengths of electric cable to be used without the resulting loss of current. Behind the engine is Pat Collins' Channel Tunnel Railway. This took the form of a real steam engine pulling up to six trucks around a circular track, at least half of which was in darkness. At the time of its inception in the late 1880s it was a great novelty, as many people had never travelled on a railway train. Because of the darkness, it was also much appreciated by young couples who made up a high percentage of the customers. This scene shows the Goose Fair at the Nottingham Market Place in 1895, with the Old Exchange in the background.

96 At each fairground, the showmen had to make sure there was an adequate supply of coal and water for the steam engines. Water was usually stored in barrels nearby or brought in by dandy or water cart. In this scene a lorry is bringing in a new supply of coal for the showman's engine before the fair gets under way; the dragons on Pat Collins' Scenic are still sheeted. While the traction engines usually burnt steam coal, the centre engines on the machines were often coke fired to reduce the risk of sparks falling from the chimney onto the canvas tilts or covers. On the right is Holland's very elaborate Scenic Whales. The engine is Fowler Number 14424 *Dreadnought* which was built to the order of the War Office during World War I and is now preserved under the name of *Goliath.* As the engine is partly standing on the pavement, the driver has levelled it with blocks to keep the boiler 'head-up'. This helps to keep the maximum amount of water back against and around the firebox.

This scene is taken from nearly the same spot as the previous picture, but from a lower vantage point and over thirty years later. It shows the Goose Fair at Nottingham in 1927, the last to be held in the Market Place before being transferred to its present site on The Forest. In the background is the steel framework for the Council House which was then being built to replace the Old Exchange.

97 Fun Fairs are popular attractions for galas and carnivals, so when Barnsley held a 'Joy Week' in Locke Park there was quite a big fair. Unfortunately, however, it took place in the wettest week of 1936, despite being held in July. The grassland site quickly became a sea of mud. When they came to depart, the stallholders hired a contractor's traction engine to extricate their living vans from the water-logged ground, paying ten shillings a time. In a very short time, however, even this engine sank deeply into the ground and it took considerable time to extricate it. This view shows Harry Hall's big Burrell *The Whale*, with chains on its driving wheels to give added grip on the soft ground. Before the days of rubber tyres, it was possible for showmen to bolt pieces of angle iron called 'spuds' direct to the metal wheels; these gave superior adhesion under such adverse conditions. It can be seen that the driving pins in the rear wheel have been pulled out, enabling the engine's winch to revolve freely so that the wire rope can be used to pull out the bogged vehicles.

In the background is a Tilling-Stevens petrol-electric truck, a great favourite with showmen. A petrol engine drove a dynamo; this powered an electric motor, which provided the final drive. Many showmen used these lorries much in the same way as a showman's engine. After the lorry had pulled the loads to the ground, the dynamo was used to provide lighting for the show.

98 Many showmen took advantage of the large number of ex-War Department lorries which came on the market after World War I. Most of these were fully reconditioned before being sold and rendered yeoman service on the fairgrounds until the late 1930s. This photograph, taken in 1923, shows an ex-WD FWD lorry towing a living van onto the tober. FWD is the maker's name; the letters stand for four wheel drive, and it can be seen that full use is being made of this with chains on all four wheels giving extra adhesion. The lorry has been converted into a packing truck and carries a heavy load.

99 Transition in transport on the fairground. Showmen arrive to set up Mitcham Fair in the late 1920s. Some of the loads have been brought in by traction engine, others by motor lorry, mainly Tilling-Stevens and AECs. The sites, rides and stalls have been marked out, and some of the packing trucks are being unloaded. On the right an Erskine car is towing a small caravan. Trailer car caravans made their appearance in 1919, one of the earliest firms in the business being Eccles who later went on to build some for showmen's use. The horses come from a travelling circus which was making up part of the show.

100 Fairgrounds were the last stronghold of the steam traction engine. Roundabout proprietors favoured them for their unfailing reliability. Further, being both big and powerful, they were capable of 'holding back' the heavy loads on gradients. John Fowler & Co (Leeds) Ltd built a special showman's diesel-engined road locomotive in 1935 for the Nottingham-based firm of Hibble & Mellors Ltd. It was appropriately named *Jubilee* because of the royal event of that year. It did not have the success anticipated, and Fowlers never built another. At that time, steam traction engines were readily available second-hand at a low price, whereas a brand-new diesel was quite an expensive item of equipment. The Fowler's ancestry is obvious from its rear wheels, which

are exactly the same as those fitted to *Supreme,* their final showman's engine built the year before. Behind the cab there is a 450/500 amp dynamo. The catalogue for this machine makes interesting reading, as it lists the many advantages of the diesel engine over the steam engine:

No driver required when generating on the fairground
No getting up steam
No picking up water on the road
No clinkering up
No plugs to drop or loss of steam at a crucial time
No washing out
No leaking tubes
No floods of water around the engine on the fairground

101 Pudding Wilson's Grand Electric Coloseum (Bioscope) in trouble at Wooler Bridge in June 1908. The engine failed to straighten up after taking a left-hand bend onto the bridge and ploughed through the parapet. Luckily, the drawbar between the engine and the first truck did not break as it was only the weight of the load which prevented the Fowler engine No 10328 *Dawn of the Century* from plunging into the river.

102 One of the most serious accidents to befall a showman's engine and road train was this one in County Durham, when the engine plunged through a wall into Park Dene valley when travelling from Burnopfield to Rowlands Gill, in 1923. The apparent carnage behind the engine has been caused by the truck containing all the animals from a set of Gallopers having burst open on impact, scattering the ride all over the valley. Unfortunately the driver of the engine was killed.

ACCIDENT AT WOOLER BRIDGE JUNE 18 1908

103 Considering the thousands of miles travelled by the fairs each year, there were very few accidents on the road. In the days of steam, when an engine with a load behind it did get out of control the results were usually spectacular. In this case a complete road train—traction engine, living van and two other trailers— has plunged off the road into the lake at Thirlmere, in June 1908, killing the driver. The Burrell Showman's Engine 2979 *Reliance* was completely submerged in the lake. This is the start of the rescue operation, with private possessions being salvaged from the living wagon. The engine involved in the accident belonged to Relph and Pedley and was only three months old. It was salvaged and sent 'in pieces' to the Thetford manufacturers who rebuilt and repaired it; it emerged as No 3038 and was renamed *The Prince* for Reuben Holdsworth's Flying Pigs and Waltzing Balloons.

104 The well known West Country Showmen Anderton & Rowland ran two fairs and a fleet of Burrell showman's engines. Here No 3833 *Queen Mary* is in trouble in the middle of Torquay, on the way to Plymouth. It skidded into a shop and blocked the road. The driver was uninjured, and there were no other casualties. The date was July 1935. The correct procedure for taking a heavy road train down a hill would be to have the brakeman apply the brakes on the loads, and then for the engine literally to pull the load down the hill against the brakes. It would appear from the form this accident has taken that the brakes were not firmly applied, and the load has tried to overtake the engine, pushing it sideways across the road, and wedging it between the shops.

103

105 Arnold Brothers' fair was one of the few which regularly travelled the Isle of Wight and they had their winter quarters there as well. This fair spent part of the year on the mainland, necessitating two crossings of the Solent every season. There were no drive-on, drive-off ferries in those days; just a train of barges towed by tugboat. Great driving skill was needed to load these barges, as everthing had to be pushed on backwards down the slipway and up a ramp onto the barge; as can be seen in this photograph taken in 1927, clearances were very small. Showmen's engines were also transported in this way, and it is interesting to see that the Chairoplane truck on the right-hand side was an even heavier item, weighing no less than twenty-two tons. Occasionally disaster struck. There are reputed to be six brand-new 1920 cars in the Solent, the result of a collision between the ferry and another ship on the Lymington-Yarmouth run. George Baker and Sons of Southampton lost a complete set of Gallopers in the same way on the rival Portsmouth-Ryde route in 1908.

106 During World War I the Government requisitioned traction engines, complete with drivers, and put them to work on official contracts. In many cases, they were involved in hauling gravel for building army camps and road making, and hauling stores from railway stations to the camps. Many showmen had their engines taken over as in this case, where W. Cole & Sons' three-speed Wallis & Steevens No 7052 *Morning Star* is being used to carry horses' fodder from Wool Station in Dorset to Bovington Camp. Though the engine still carries its showman's lettering on the canopy, the dynamo has been removed in the interests of lightness.

Living Waggons

107 The showman's waggon was his home; though some of the wealthier ones might have houses to live in during the winter, almost without exception they travelled in caravans while on the road. A simple waggon might have cost as little as £100, but the average price must have been nearer £1,000. Originally, as in this pre-World War I example, they were designed to be pulled by horses. Due to the relatively poor state of the roads, they had large wooden wheels. Both inside and outside would be highly decorated, the showmen developing their own folk art in much the same way as the gypsies or canal boatmen. Braking is only on the rear wheels and the brake shoe (which operates on the metal tyre) is plainly visible.

108 Some vans were so highly decorated that the paintwork had to be protected from the sun in the summer by canvas sheeting hung down over the sides, as in this example in the 1920s. In many cases, this sheeting was only lifted on very special occasions to show the splendours of the highly varnished paintwork and gold leaf underneath. Note the beautiful cut-glass windows. The clerestory roof, sometimes known as a 'Mollycroft', gave greater headroom throughout the centre of the van and extra windows for ventilation. As with a modern caravan, they had to be level when stationary and the means of packing them up is clearly shown.

109 The showman's caravan or living waggon was his home. Some were really opulent such as William Murphy's van built by Orton and Spooner, which was over thirty feet long and weighed ten tons. Superbly panelled, it had an electric fire and electric radiators as well. When on the road all the ornaments, vases and other loose equipment had to be stowed away carefully in lockers to prevent breakages. The showman's wife was continually building up and taking down her own home.

110 Usually the main source of heating in a van was a 'Hostess' or similar stove. On this all cooking and baking would be done, no doubt using coal which was intended for the showman's engine! Heaps of coal by the traction engine used to be sadly depleted, so Yorkshire showman Mr Waddington had his stock-pile whitewashed in an attempt to put a stop to 'coal pinching'. When one of the fair visitors asked why, Mr Waddington told him that he didn't want clouds of black smoke going into peoples' eyes!

111 Cooking was seldom done out of doors, but here at a northern fair around 1910 we see that the 'Hostess' has been taken outside and is in use at the back of one of the shows. Drinking water was a problem at any fair, the showmen having to carry it in large containers such as the galvanised one on the left. Nowadays these are often of polished stainless steel or have been chromium plated.

112 Barnet Fair in 1919 saw a large and varied collection of living waggons. Most of these are still horse-drawn, some being very simple affairs while others show the wealth of their owners. None appear to be fitted with the outside kitchen which became common when solid fuel stoves for heating and cooking gave way to paraffin and primus stoves for cooking only. It would also appear that some of the canvas-covered packing trucks were used by the gaff lads for sleeping quarters. Where a waggon had no windows on one side, if often meant that the van would be used as the backwall of a sideshow, such as a Shooter.

112

113 Funerals of fairground travellers are always attended by large numbers of relatives and friends, many of whom travel great distances in order to pay their last respects. Floral tributes are invariably numerous and beautiful. Reports of such funerals often occupy many columns in the showman's weekly newspaper *The World's Fair*. Often a caravan would remain empty for a long time after a funeral before the family settled into it again. In some cases it might even be sold and another one bought instead.

114 While the packing truck was primarily designed for moving the various loads of the fair on the road, it could also double up as sleeping quarters for some of the workmen. This Swinging Boat packing truck belonged to Arnold Brothers and contained living quarters for up to six hands. It carried 102 pieces belonging to the Swinging Boat, all the poles for a Coconut Sheet, a complete darts stall, a skittle stall, a round stall and a small arcade, plus ladder, steps and ball boxes, and is seen at Mill Hill, Cowes, Isle of Wight in 1932.

Permanent Fairground Sites

2.217. GENERAL VIEW OF THE PLEASURE BEACH

115 The traditional site for the permanent amusement park is at one of the popular seaside resorts, where the fair is often situated very close to the beach, as here at Great Yarmouth. Showmen who do not have travelling in their blood prefer this type of site. The takings are steady and they do not have the problems associated with moving about and continual building up and pulling down. Some seaside sites allow the rides to stay built up all through the year; others have to be cleared each autumn. Here we see, in the background, a Mountain Glide and a compact Figure of Eight version of the Big Dipper. In the foreground is a Heyday, a version of the Swirl or Whip, where series of spinning cars are propelled around a centre platform and allowed to skid outwards on the corners. The rider had no control over the cars but often the moneytakers would give cars a hefty push to build up more swing. On the right is a slot-machine arcade, something more often associated with the seaside and the pier than with travelling fairs.

116 The permanent amusement park allows the showman much more scope for his rides and machines. They can be much larger than those of the travelling fair, and do not have to be regularly dismantled. The British Empire Exhibition, Wembley, held in 1924, the like of which is unlikely to be seen again, was such a tremendous success that it remained open for another year. The Amusement Park was a real highlight and proved immensely popular, its skyline dominated by his great Racer, more often known as the Big Dipper. Patrons travelled in cars, sometimes singly or, as in this case, in trains. The cars were transported up to the top of the ride by a moving rack system, and then

let go. Often they continued only by gravity, the downward speed being enough to take them over the next hump. On some of the longer rides they were again assisted up some of the steeper slopes. The space under the racer is also well employed; in the foreground was the River Caves, an underground trip by boat through artificial grottos.

117 One of the attractions often to be found on the permanent amusement site is the Miniature Railway. Here at the Great Exhibition at Wembley we see a typical example. Though in this case the Railway was sponsored during the Exhibition by the Canadian Pacific Railway, the engines and

rolling stock were decidedly British. The engine is a $9\frac{1}{4}$in gauge Great Northern Atlantic originally operating on a line at Staughton Manor, owned by J.E.P. Howey who, with Count Louis Zborowski, founded the Romney, Hythe & Dymchurch Railway in Kent. The late J.A. Holder bought the engine in 1925 and operated it at Wembley as the Treasure Island Railway. The name of the engine at that time was *Peter Pan.* Later in life the engine ran on a private railway on the author's home territory at Beaulieu. The owner, Terence Holder, who is seen driving in this photograph, is still actively connected with steam preservation on the Dart Valley Railway.

EARLS COURT. THE GREAT WHEEL. 3964.   L.S.&P.Co.

118 One of the largest Big Wheels ever erected in this country was built at Earls Court, London, for the Exhibition of 1894. It was known, not unnaturally, as the Great Wheel. It had no less than forty cars and could carry two hundred people; the problems of loading and unloading the cars can be imagined. It was driven by two 50hp motors and measured 280ft in diameter. A similar wheel was erected in Vienna.

119 The Kursaal has long been the playground of Londoners visiting Southend-on-Sea. Here, in 1921, we see patrons enjoying the Tubs—a circular ride on which the Tubs are propelled around the centre of the machine with the top part of the Tub containing the patron, being made to spin by contact with the inside walls. As can be seen, the Tubs can also tilt. The notices or 'gag cards' are a good example of methods used to attract patrons to a ride. One would have thought that it would have been most uncomfortable to have a 'spoon by the light of the moon' on a revolving tilting Tub.

120 One of the most unusual machines at the Wembley Exhibition in 1924, was called the Whirl of the World. Here, discs revolved within the floor, spinning in different directions, so throwing the riders in their small cars away in different directions. A certain amount of braking and steering could be undertaken by the rider with the aid of the centre lever.

121 One of the most impressive machines ever to be presented on any British fairground was the Flying Machine. This was a much grander version of the Chairoplanes and could only be built up on a permanent site. The holiday makers rode in suspended cars, rather like the gondolas of an airship. This is the holiday resort of Southport in 1909. On the left is a water chute; the thrill of hurtling down the slope and hitting the water in a huge spray can be imagined. On some similar rides, spectators could view the cars hitting the water in close-up from behind a plate-glass window. Most of these spectators would scream and instinctively duck when they saw the bow-wave from the boat approaching them. The glass barrier of course kept them dry.

Index